THE AMERICAN CHURCH.

A

DISCOURSE

IN BEHALF OF THE

American Home Missionary Society,

PREACHED IN THE CITIES OF NEW YORK AND BROOKLYN,

MAY, 1852.

BY

REV. LEONARD BACON, D.D.,

PASTOR OF THE FIRST CHURCH IN NEW HAVEN, CONN

NEW YORK:

PRINTED FOR THE AMERICAN HOME MISSIONARY SOCIETY,

BY BAKER, GODWIN & CO., NO. 1 SPRUCE STREET.

1852.

DISCOURSE.

TITUS 1: 5.

THAT THOU SHOULDST SET IN ORDER THE THINGS THAT ARE WANTING, AND ORDAIN ELDERS IN EVERY CITY, AS I HAD APPOINTED THEE.

This, and some other passages of the same sort, describe one essential point in the primitive propagation of the Gospel. The Apostles and their associates went everywhere, preaching the word, reasoning out of the Scriptures in the synagogues of Judaism, and disputing, if they had opportunity, in the schools of Gentile philosophy. But this was not all. They baptized individuals and households, on a profession of faith in Jesus Christ as the Son of God and the Savior of the world—thus marking a line of distinction between the holy commonwealth of the redeemed and the world of the unbelieving. But this was not all. They wrote books and tracts, giving them such publication and currency as was then practicable; thus putting upon record, for all nations and for all ages, the great facts and elementary principles which they were commissioned to promulgate. But this was not all. There was another step to be taken, without which Christianity would hardly have had a place in history. Up to this point, if their work be regarded as ending at this point, all their results are incomplete—the half-collected materials of a structure—

the dissevered parts and members, on the one hand, but not compacted into symmetry and strength; the living spirit, on the other hand, but not embodied as an organic force, with a local habitation and a name. "For this cause," says Paul the Apostle to Titus the Evangelist, "left I thee in Crete, that thou shouldst set in order the things that are wanting, and ordain elders in every city, as I had appointed thee."

In the great island of Crete, Paul seems to have labored in person, and he seems to have been interrupted and called away before the ordinary plan of his operations had been carried out. Some arrangements were still wanting, which Titus was expected to supply. In every town or local community where converts had been made, he was to organize the Christian fellowship by instituting elders, the proper officers of a stated worshiping assembly. In other words, the work for which the Apostle had left him in Crete was that of constituting local churches, and so completing the introduction of the Gospel there. The same thing was done wherever the Apostles performed their office. By the establishment of churches—local Christian societies for worship and for religious instruction and discipline—Christianity became something more than a matter of individual opinion, conviction and experience; something more than a merely domestic influence, hallowing in God's name the relations of household love and duty; something more than a new element infused into literature and philosophy, and taking effect upon the progress of human intelligence from age to age. It became an incorporated and organized religion, with its own arrangements and institutions for self-perpetuation, and for aggressive influence. Christianity establishing itself in local churches, became a new social institute within the State, yet not of it; a new order and form of human association, with an independent life of its own and yet connected by a relation of constant action and reaction with that old order of things into which it had been cast.

The American Home Missionary Society devotes itself to a work of the same kind with that for which Titus was left in Crete. It has for its own special department of effort, on the broad field of Christian activity in our country, not merely the work of diffusing Christian knowledge, not merely the work of winning individuals to personal faith in Christ, not merely the work of multiplying and sending abroad the living preachers of the Gospel, but the work of planting Christianity as an organized religion and an organizing power. Books, however excellent, and however profusely distributed; the itinerant and desultory preaching of the Gospel, whether by book-venders and tract distributors, or by professional and authenticated ministers of the word; Sunday-schools, with their apparatus of libraries, teachers and traveling missionaries, may co-operate powerfully for the advancement of Christian knowledge and experience; but such efforts, if they are all, work no organic change in society. Another kind of effort must accompany them, or follow them, to "set in order the things that are wanting," or else, so far as permanent influence is concerned, their labor is in vain.

Allow me to say, in this place, that, in respect to ecclesiastical arrangements, the Home Missionary enterprise, as represented by the Society for which this service is performed, is not a sectarian undertaking. It attempts nothing more than to establish local churches —churches in the New Testament sense of the word—

organized parochial societies of Christian people, for the support of public worship, and for the various duties of Christian neighborhood and communion. With the internal arrangements of these churches for the management of their own ecclesiastical affairs, with the relations which associated churches may see fit to establish among themselves for the sake of mutual recognition and intercourse, or of mutual helpfulness and authority, it does not intermeddle. The particular church may or may not conduct its own affairs on purely democratic principles; it may or may not incorporate itself with some larger and more comprehensive organization; the Home Missionary Society does not concern itself with such questions. The plan of our great charity is essentially opposed to the denominational or sectarian spirit. So long as the churches which it plants, or which it aids in the period of their weakness, are evangelical in worship and doctrine, holding that view of the Christian system of which the word *evangelical* has become, in modern times, the recognized and current designation; so long as they are essentially self-governed, and not priest-governed; so long as they do not formally exclude from fellowship with them the great body of churches on which this charity depends for its resources, so long it cares not what regulations and arrangements, or what denominational standards may be adopted by any particular congregation. It has to do, not with the extension of organized sects or denominations, but only with single churches, local churches. As a purely American institution, called into existence by an exigency in the growth of this great American people, and operating to extend the dominion of Christ over all the territory of our Union, it devotes itself to the one work of setting up Christianity in the form of local Christian churches, that shall operate from age to age upon the character and destiny of the countless millions of our population.

Thus there opens before us, at this point, a great subject of thought and inquiry:

THE CHRISTIAN INSTITUTION OF LOCAL CHURCHES AS RELATED TO OUR AMERICAN CIVILIZATION.

I feel that the subject has its difficulties. I am fully conscious that I shall not succeed in giving it such illustration as it deserves. But I am sure that even an imperfect illustration of it will help us to some new views of the position which this Home Missionary work ought to have in our affections and in our plans of patriotic and Christian beneficence.

I. Let me remind you, then, that religion, embodied in religious institutions, is an essential and potent element in every form of civilization. Religion, in the generic sense of the word—the consciousness of dependence on an invisible and infinite Power—is not only an inseparable part of our human nature, belonging, like reason and the faculty of moral perception, to the constitution of every individual mind; it is also, like them, essential to the constitution of society. It has to do with all human relations, but most of all with those complicated relations of man to man which constitute the conscious unity of the commonwealth, and by virtue of which the life of the State runs on in undying and uninterrupted identity through successive generations of individual mortal existence. Though religion is in one sense wholly individual; though true religion, considered as a religious experience, is the awakening of the individual man to a just view of the relations between himself and his Maker; it is none the less true, that the religious instincts and sensibilities are developed in society. They have their place and their activity in connection with every social affection and every social duty, giving a sanction from the Infinite to all the complicated relationships which hold society together, and connecting the visible and transient, at every point of human life, with the invisible and the eternal. They are eminently sympathetic, yearning after communion, unfolding and strengthening themselves in the consciousness of fellowship; so that some form of religion, not merely as a private personal conviction, but as a social institution, with public or social worship, is a necessity of human nature. Thus they take their shape and direction from social influences; and in one form and another they are incorporated into the character and historic life of nations and races. Thus all history is full of the influence of religion as a leading element of civilization. Of this it may be a sufficient illustration to say that in every land that ever had a history, the great architectural remains and monuments, from which, more perhaps than from any historic records, we learn the extent and the distinctive character of the civilization which once flourished there, are remains of religious architecture. The colossal structures of Egypt; the august colonnades of Baalbec and Palmyra; the disinhumed remains of Assyria; the stupendous excavations and sculptured mountains of India; the old, rude columns on Salisbury Plain; the fantastic mounds reared by an unknown race upon the soil which now we call our own, all testify to the power of the religious principle in human nature, and to the invariableness of its presence as an element in every form of civilization. And how plainly does history, in its records, teach us that the introduction of a new religion, into any country, carries into the civilization of that country a consequent and proportionate change.

II. Turning now to recollect for a moment the distinctive characteristics of our American civilization, and to inquire how it differs from the civilization of other ages, and from the existing civilization of other countries, we find, at the first glance, certain great outlines sufficiently definite for our present use. We see an entire separation of religion from the jurisdiction of the civil magistrate, and an absolute freedom of voluntary association for worship, and for all religious purposes. We see the religious element everywhere at work; the people everywhere organizing and sustaining their religious institutions altogether independent of the civil government, which also they organize and sustain. We see the principle of local and municipal self-government carried to the greatest practicable extent, in opposition to the centralization of power. We see an equality of personal and political rights, such as has never existed elsewhere, and, growing out of it, a constantly counteracted but ever elastic tendency to equality of condition. We see an unparalleled diffusion of intelligence and of the spirit of inquiry and free thought, stimulated continually by the genius and the working of our political institutions. We see twenty-five millions of people, spread over a territory of various and boundless resources, and trained to the habit of relying on themselves rather than on the government for guidance and control, and of exercising their own faculties of thought and judgment on matters of public, not less than of private interest. We see this teeming population increasing every year by a stupendous immigration from all regions of the ancient world; the immigrant myriads bringing with them from beyond the ocean their own languages and fashions, and their own forms of religion or of irreligion, yet mingling with the mighty mass, unable to resist its tendencies, and slowly but surely losing their foreign peculiarities,—as the waters of the Mississippi, poured into the Gulf and the Atlantic, and slowly mingling with the rolling tides, lose their freshness, deposit the soil that they have brought from distant plains and mountains, and are gradually lost and undistinguishable in the world-embracing ocean, without discoloring by one shade or turbid stain its boundless azure.

III. And now, with these views of religion as a necessary element in every form of civilization, and with these views of the peculiarities by which our American civilization is distinguished, we may take the position that in our country, and under our social and civil organization, the strength of free and Protestant Christianity, considered as an organized religion and an organizing power, must reside in local and self-governed churches. To illustrate this, let me point out to your attention certain facts and views, which show what local churches have been in the progress of our history to the present moment, and what they are likely to be in the future.

1. It is worthy of notice that the history of the origin and progress of Christian institutions in this country, hitherto, is almost wholly bound up in the history of the origin and growth of local churches. In New England, as you are well aware,—which has had by its religious and political institutions, and by the character which those institutions have wrought into its

people, so wide an influence upon the political and religious organization of the country as a whole—the institution of local churches, self-constituted and self-governed, was at first the end for which every thing else was instituted. The Puritan emigration from old England was an emigration for the express purpose of founding in the wilderness local, separate, independent churches, which should control the founding of every thing else; and around which, as so many distinct centers of vital power, there should arise the laws and magistracies, the order, the industry, the justice, the popular virtue, the universal education and intelligence, the frugal plenty, and all the stern and saintly beauty of a Puritan civilization. Whatever there is in New England that warms the heart of the New Englander with glad and reverent affection at the thought of her gray rocks and her green hillsides, when his filial regards turn eastward from the prairies, or from beyond the Rocky Mountains,—is most intimately associated with the influence of those New England churches. Whatever errors there may have been in the ancient legislation there, whatever violations of the principle of religious liberty, whatever unwise attempts to make men religious, and to keep them in right ways of thinking by the force of law, there was never in those Puritan commonwealths a centralization of ecclesiastical power; never a priestly corporation independent of the people; never any religious organization higher or stronger than that of local churches; and at this moment all the embodied and organized religious influence there is summed up in the fact, that in every township, and in every parochial district, the local church is present, the organized congregation of free Christian men, the self-governed Christian society, with its stated worship, with its house of prayer, with its teaching ministry, and with all its apparatus of instruction and influence.

But I would not be understood as speaking of that particular form of church-order which is called Congregationalism, or as claiming for the churches thus denominated a special advantage, in this respect, over churches bearing other names. What was the origin of Presbyterianism on our soil? It did not begin here, as it began under the hands of the Reformers in Scotland, in a General Assembly, distributing and parceling itself out into synods and presbyteries, and ending in the organization of parochial arrangements. On the contrary, it began in local, separate, Presbyterian congregations, each with its own arrangements for worship, discipline, and the ministry of the word; and it was the voluntary confederation of congregations previously independent of each other, which gave being to presbyteries, synods, and general assemblies. So with other churches of similar faith and order, but of a different genealogy—the Reformed Dutch, the German Reformed, the Lutheran,—trace their history back to its earliest sources, and, in each instance, you find a particular congregation in one place, and another particular congregation in another place, and then another and another, till at last these many congregations, drawn together by special affinities of faith and order, of ancestral feeling and perhaps of language, are confederated for mutual helpfulness in classical and synodical assemblies. But in all these instances, and even in others which are very unlike to these in some respects, but of which I could not speak without entering into explanations which the limits of this discourse preclude, the strength of the organization, its efficiency in maintaining and extending the kingdom of Christ, and especially the efficiency with which it dispenses the Gospel, as a vital and organizing force in society, molding the character of the people; the efficacy with which it works to carry into households, and into the experience of individual souls, the light and life of holiness, must be found, not in its supposed or attempted centralization of power, but in the strength, the number, and the spiritual health and activity of its local churches. And to a thinking, generous, Christian mind, the value of all these ecclesiastical confederations, by whatever name they may be called, and whatever may be the theory on which they are constituted, lies in their ability to subserve the true interests, and to promote the legitimate efficiency, of parochial churches, and to provide for the multiplication of such churches in a just proportion to the wants of the population. The presbytery, the consociation, the classis, the convention, the synod, is for the churches; not the churches for it. Its strength is not in itself, but in the churches whose confederation has created it. Its value is measured exactly by what it contributes to their edification and efficiency. If the churches which it includes are, by virtue of their relation to it, more peaceful, more prosperous, more potent in their local influence, then it answers a legitimate and important purpose, and deserves to be honored accordingly. But if, instead of this, the churches gather from it only a thorny harvest of strife and debate; or if it becomes a mere arena for feats of logical and theological gladiatorship, then, let Diotrephes admire it and rejoice in it as he may, it answers no good end, and forfeits its right to existence.

Pardon the desultory character of these remarks. They are intended to illustrate, and, if I mistake not, they do illustrate the position that Protestant Evangelical Christianity upon this American soil is identified, in its beginning and growth, and in its present position and influence, with the origin and progress, the prosperity and efficiency of local churches. Perhaps I have said more than enough; and yet I cannot refrain from adding, that if any intelligent and impartial man will set himself to study the institutions of this great metropolis, he will find that not the colleges, nor even the public schools, not the learned academies, nor the charitable institutions, nor even the diversified apparatus of extra-ecclesiastical religious enterprise, can be compared in importance with the churches, the natural depositaries, the legitimate conservators and dispensers of all Christian influence. And when he takes his census of the churches, and sums up their power, and makes his estimate of their capabilities, he will think of them only as so many organized congregations of Christian worshipers, with their pastors and other officers, their sabbaths, their places of public worship, their lecture-rooms, their Sunday-schools, their meetings for edification and brotherly communion, their arrangements for aggressive action on the masses of ignorance and impiety that lie around them; and he will take no account of presbyteries or associations, of classes or synods, unless it be for convenience in the prosecution of his inquiries, and the summing up of his results. This very church, for example, in whose consecrated edifice we are this evening assembled, how shall we estimate its importance as one of the institutions of this metropolis? This house of prayer, these Sabbath assemblies, the sacred tie that binds these congregated households to each other, the covenant of baptism, the remembered blood that bought our pardon, the eloquence on themes of infinite grandeur that has here distilled from lips touched with the fire of God's own altar, the impressions and experiences that have taken place within these walls, the decisions that have been formed here for eternity, the consolation that, in connection with these ministrations, has been poured into the bosom of affliction, the rainbow-splendor with which hope here nurtured has so often overarched the river of death, the great thoughts and emotions that have here been born and cherished in believing souls and that have gone out hence to be translated into godlike action, the mischievous influences that have been counteracted from this center, the wanderers that have been reclaimed, the outcasts that have been saved, the miseries that have been alleviated,—Oh how can we conceive of the infinite history! And all this influence is the influence of—what? A single, organized, local congregation, taken by itself. Who, when he attempts to estimate this influence, and when his heart swells with the thought that there is such an institution, and that this is only a specimen of what churches are doing for the moral welfare of this great metropolis, can think of asking to which presbytery the church belongs, or whether it belongs to any? How completely would any such question let us down from the altitude at which we see the church itself in its legitimate and blessed influence!

2. And now, though we begin to feel the narrowness of our limits as to time, let me lead you to inquire whether it is not a fact, that in all ecclesiastical organizations within the scope of our American civilization, there is a steady tendency toward the increase of what we may call the parochial element in ecclesiastical order, as opposed to the element of consolidation. I have called your attention to the fact that the history of

Protestant Evangelical Christianity among us is to a great extent, when rightly viewed, the history of local churches, as local centers of evangelical influence upon the people; but now I wish to lead you to a wider view. The tendency to the increase of this parochial element of church-order, cannot be easily measured by a reference to those religious bodies in which the parochial element has always been predominant. There is, however, a powerful evangelical body, the history of which is in some respects singularly contrasted with that of the various churches to which I have already made particular allusion. I speak of that body here with no sentiment that is not consistent with the profoundest respect for its Christian and evangelical character. I thank God for the Methodist Episcopal Church in these United States. I thank God for that wonderful system of evangelism which has done so much for the advancement of our common Christianity, and which gives promise of so glorious an usefulness in the future. But what is it which that great itineracy is everywhere accomplishing? What are its achievements as a permanent and organizing influence in society? How is its usefulness to be measured upon the scale of history? Wherever it works, it is working to form permanent congregations, local, organized churches, as fixed centers of local influence. And do we not see that the Methodist house of worship, after a little while, is no longer a mere preaching station? The benches are displaced by pews; the original division of the assembly is superseded by a distribution into households; the itinerant preacher, who hastened from one station to another, has become a temporary pastor; and presently the congregation, trained from the first to an intense religious activity, begins to be conscious of its corporate unity, and of its duties, and its rights too, as a local, Christian church. It is not for me to prognosticate the issue of a pending debate. It is not for us in this place to intermeddle with affairs that are not our own. But may we not confidently expect, from the deep sagacity that has characterized the progress of that religious body heretofore, and from the evident blessing with which God has attended it, that whatever may be the immediate result, the end will be, not conflict, not disorganization and confusion, but such an adjustment as shall provide more adequately for the development of the parochial element of church-order, without impairing the aggressive force of that system of evangelism?

We might take a still wider view. The Roman Catholic system has long been struggling to establish itself in this country. Having to do almost exclusively with the foreign element in our population, as distinguished from the people that have been born and trained under purely American influences, it has hardly begun to feel, as yet, the forces that are destined ere long to act upon it. But is there any intelligent observer who is not aware that in the bosom of that great system of spiritual despotism, as it exists among us, there are already some movements significant of what will be hereafter. A Roman Catholic congregation of American citizens, born and nurtured on the soil, and in the atmosphere of our national life,—nay, a Roman Catholic congregation with only an infusion of the true spirit of American civilization,—when once it begins to be conscious of something like a corporate unity, begins to be strangely conscious of corporate rights and corporate duties.

There is meaning in this. Wherever it appears, it is a phenomenon which invites an inquiry into the reason of it. And the reason of it is found in the congruity between the parochial principle of religious organization, and that principle of local and municipal self-government which is the grand distinction of our political system, and which is most thoroughly carried out where our political system exists in its most perfect and compacted form; which is where the territory of the State, after having been divided into counties, is again divided into townships, and where the inhabitants of every town are a complete local democracy, enacting their own by-laws in popular assemblies, choosing their own magistrates, taking care of their own free roads and free schools, and having a part by their own town-representative in the legislation of the State.

IV. May we not come, then, to this conclusion: That which we have seen to be the Protestant Evangelical form of church-order, the system of parochial churches, each a local center of all Christian influences, is essential to the right and successful working of our great principle of local self-government in the civil state. Our entire system of social organization—the entire genius of our people expressing itself in political institutions—dreads and abhors the centralization of power, refuses to collect the majesty of government into any one imperial locality, sets up everywhere the municipal, local democracy, and insists that the people, at every point at which a political body can be constituted, shall attend to their own business of governing themselves. In such a structure and system of society, the only religious principle, so far as order and organization are concerned—the only principle, I mean, that is in harmony with the genius of the people, or that can adjust itself without conflict or collision to all the machinery of their political life—is the principle of parochial and self-governed churches. This is the distinctively American method of religious organization. The people—a Christian people in their descent and history, in their language and literature, in their recognized standards of morality, and in their ideas of God, and of the worship which men owe to their Creator—are the State; as such they organize themselves for political and civil purposes under the forms of a free self-government, resting on the basis of municipal institutions universally distributed; and this is the American political system. The same people, acting in reference to their religious wants and sympathies, organize themselves everywhere, voluntarily and according to a Christian freedom, in stated assemblies for worship and religious instruction; and this is *the American church system.* The Church and the State are everywhere present to each other, and everywhere mutually dependent. Each system is complete in itself, yet each is intimately related to the other, and to the living whole of which they are the living parts. There is no rivalry between them, no clashing of jurisdictions, no conflict of powers, no subordination of one to the other. The State everywhere protects the Church from outrage, recognizes its rights by recognizing and maintaining the right of free association for religious purposes, guards every worshiping assembly against disturbance, hallows by law the Christian Sabbath as the people's day of rest, inaugurates its own proceedings in legislative assemblies, and often in courts of justice, with religious services, conducted according to the order of the local churches. So, in return, the Church everywhere gives life to the State; everywhere it penetrates with its vital force all the municipal livisions and arrangements of the commonwealth,—as the nervous system in the human frame is spread through every limb and organ, every muscle, every fibre, the vehicle of life and sense and motion; everywhere, if adequately developed, it works upon the common mind and life of the people, keeping alive the sense of relations to the invisible and the remembrance of truths that reach beyond the sphere of sense and time. And this parochial, self-organizing principle of evangelical Christianity, everywhere present; everywhere building the house of prayer; everywhere providing the ministry of the life-giving word; everywhere touching the most sacred springs of human sympathy, by exhibiting the simple symbolic rites of Christian faith and worship; everywhere establishing its order, its discipline, its multiform activity; and thus acting everywhere with a steady, molding influence on the sentiments and habits of the people, trains the people into the capacity of self-government. It deals with them from their childhood as intelligent and reasonable beings, and as capable of acting under the excitement and guidance of the sublimest motives. It holds them to the duty of exercising their own faculties of thought and judgment on themes of infinite reach and grandeur. It makes them familiar with the consciousness of a responsibility to God, which rises far above all other responsibilities, and includes them all, and from which no considerations of personal or worldly expediency can absolve them. It teaches them in these methods the grand lesson of free and manly thoughtfulness, and of free and manly self-control. Accustoming them in their various religious communities to discuss and regulate, under one form or another, and in one degree or another, their own religious affairs, by yielding a generous deference to the judgment and the choice of the majority, it trains them for political freedom and for self-government, as members of the civil commonwealth. How happy the lot, how beautiful the aspect, of a great people whose institutions, thus organized in Church and State, spring as it were spontaneously from the tendencies and yearnings of the popular mind, and are adapted to the ends for which the Church and State exist in their harmonious co-operation—the Church and the State each resting on the basis of local self-government, and each the complement but neither the servant of the other—the people, self-governed in all their communities, free because they are Christian, and Christian because they are free!

But if we reverse this view, and instead of Protestant Evangelical Christianity establishing itself in those institutions of local self-government which are so congruous to its nature, suppose the ascendency of a different system, establishing itself, according to its nature, in the form of a consolidated spiritual despotism, how different will be the result! Look at that system, with the gigantic efforts which it is making to achieve for itself dominion on this hallowed soil. What if it shall gain in these broad realms of freedom the ascendency at which it aims, and for which it is drawing, as it were, to one center all the forces of fraud, cunning, wealth and organization, that can be wielded by the rulers of the darkness of this world? Let that system conquer; let its institutions, with no local self-governed Christian assemblies, become the predominant religious organization throughout our country; let it have, undisputed, the religious training of the people; let it teach the American citizen everywhere to bow in awe before the divine authority of the priesthood, to forego the keeping of his own conscience, to renounce his right of judging for himself under the guidance of God's word and Spirit, and in the discharge of his personal responsibility to God; let it succeed in molding the hearts and habits of the people, by the action of its institutions, into accordance with its own despotic genius, and how completely will it counteract all the better tendencies, and extinguish the characteristic spirit of our existing American civilization.

With such an enemy working against us—an enemy so powerful in his resources, so unwearied in his diligence, and so deadly in his hostility to all that we value for ourselves, or hope for in behalf of our children, and our country, and the world—we are to "set in order the things that are wanting," and to spread the organized form and organizing spirit of free and pure Christianity, from beautiful New England, from this imperial New York, from the Atlantic shore adorned with cities to which the commerce of the world brings riches, westward through the disappearing forests, westward over the prairies, westward still, beyond the mountains so soon to be pierced and threaded by the iron path of commerce, westward, even to where our remotest west, in its golden pride, looking forth upon the Pacific, confronts the farthest and eldest orient, and is already making China and India tributary to the greatness of its future. How inspiring is the thought of effort and achievement in such a field! "Time's noblest empire," with resources that shame the riches of the world, with capabilities of power and progress that defy all calculation, and with a position of pre-eminent grandeur, in relation to the destinies of the human race, is to be saved from the dominion of darkness and of sin, and is to be filled with the freedom of the sons of God!

This, then, is the work of the American Home Missionary Society. It undertakes to carry the Gospel with all its quickening and sanctifying influences, the Gospel, with its institutions and social order, the Gospel, not only as the offer of Divine grace to the individual soul, but also as an organizing power in the commonwealth, through all the length and breadth of this great empire. Wherever it goes, it puts its hand to the foundation, and helps to shape the structure of society. It does not merely scatter the seed of the word here and there in the wide and tangled wilderness; its work is to subdue the wilderness, to spread new order over its neglected vastness, to change its gloomy waste into the garden of the Lord. Where various currents of population, from the north and from the south, from the old world and from the new, with habits and tendencies as diverse as their origin, meet to mingle and be confounded, it sets up in that confusion of influences an organic self-perpetuating force that shall act upon unborn generations; and where the pioneer might, perhaps, have left to his posterity an inheritance of barbarism, it spreads over the subdued and renovated soil the light, the bloom, the living and perennial beauty of a Christian civilization.

www.ingramcontent.com/pod-product-compliance
Lightning Source LLC
LaVergne TN
LVHW011145110826
845150LV00008B/2514
9781418192327